Italy

Julie McCulloch

Heinemann

www.heinemann.co.uk
Visit our website to find out more information about **Heinemann Library** books.

To order:
☎ Phone 44 (0) 1865 888066
🖹 Send a fax to 44 (0) 1865 314091
💻 Visit the Heinemann Bookshop at www.heinemann.co.uk to browse our catalogue and order online.

First published in Great Britain by Heinemann Library, Halley Court, Jordan Hill, Oxford OX2 8EJ, a division of Reed Educational and Professional Publishing Ltd. Heinemann is a registered trademark of Reed Educational & Professional Publishing Limited.

OXFORD MELBOURNE AUCKLAND JOHANNESBURG BLANTYRE
GABORONE IBADAN PORTSMOUTH NH (USA) CHICAGO

Designed by Tinstar Design (www.tinstar.co.uk)
Illustrations by Nicholas Beresford-Davies
Originated by Dot Gradations
Printed by Wing King Tong in Hong Kong.

ISBN 0 431 11700 4 (hardback)   ISBN 0 431 11707 1 (paperback)
06 05 04 03 02   06 05 04 03 02
10 9 8 7 6 5 4 3 2   10 9 8 7 6 5 4 3 2 1

British Library Cataloguing in Publication Data
McCulloch, Julie
    Italy. – (A world of recipes)
    1. Cookery, Italian – Juvenile literature 2.Italy –
    Description and travel – Juvenile literature
    I. Title
    641.5'123'0945

Acknowledgements
The Publishers would like to thank the following for permission to reproduce photographs:
Robert Harding, p.5. All other photographs: Gareth Boden.
Illustration p.45, US Department of Agriculture/US Department of Health and Human Services.

Cover photographs reproduced with permission of Gareth Boden.

Our thanks to Magimix™ for the use of their equipment on pp. 13 and 36.

Our thanks to Sue Townsend, home economist, and Sue Mildenhall for their comments in the preparation of this book.

Every effort has been made to contact copyright holders of any material reproduced in this book. Any omissions will be rectified in subsequent printings if notice is given to the Publisher.

Words appearing in the text in bold, **like this**, are explained in the glossary.

Contents

Key

* easy

** medium

*** difficult

Italian food

Italy is a long, narrow country in southern Europe. Italian cooking is very popular. Some dishes, such as lasagne and ice cream, are made all over the world. Their recipes are included in this book.

In the past

Cooking in Italy is very varied. It has been influenced by people from other countries who have settled there in the past.

For example, in the 8th century BC, parts of Italy were occupied by the ancient Greeks. The Greeks introduced their foods and ways of cooking, including using flat bread, which may have led to the creation of the pizza.

Between the 1st and the 5th centuries AD, Rome, in Italy, was the centre of the huge **Roman Empire**. The Romans introduced Italian cooking to their people.

At different times between 1400 and 1700, people from France, Spain and Germany all ruled parts of Italy. Each brought their own food traditions.

Around the country

The climate and the soil in Italy are very varied. Many sorts of **grains**, fruit and vegetables are grown. Italy has a long coastline too, so plenty of fresh fish and seafood is used in Italian cooking.

The top of Italy is covered by huge mountains called the Alps. In the north, wheat, maize and rice grow on the rich farmland. People use these crops in traditional northern Italian dishes such as risotto (made from rice) and polenta (a type of flour made from maize, which can be baked or grilled).

▲ *Many people in Italy like to buy fresh fruit and vegetables from market stalls like these.*

Southern Italy is dry and rocky. Many farmers in this area grow olives both for eating and pressing to make olive oil. Traditional southern Italian dishes include pasta and pizza.

Italian meals

The main meal in Italy is usually eaten in the middle of the day, and is made up of three courses. The first course is often a rice or pasta dish. A typical main course would contain meat, chicken or fish. The meal would then be rounded off with a dessert.

Ingredients

olive oil mozzarella Dolcelatte

goats' cheese

canned tomatoes

tomatoes

dried pasta

basil

thyme

Parmesan cheese

garlic

arborio rice

rice

Because Italian cooking is so popular, most ingredients are easy to find in shops and supermarkets.

Cheese

Italians use lots of cheese in their cooking. Four different kinds of Italian cheese are used in this book: Parmesan, mozzarella, Dolcelatte and goats' cheese. Parmesan is very hard, and is usually used finely **grated** or thinly **sliced**. You can buy it ready-grated, but it tastes fresher if you buy a small block and grate it when you need it. Mozzarella is a soft, mild cheese which is used to top pizzas, and in other dishes. Dolcelatte is a blue cheese, with a strong flavour. There are lots of different sorts of goats' cheese, too, made from goats' milk.

Garlic

Garlic is used in many Italian dishes. You can buy garlic in the vegetable section of any shop or supermarket.

Herbs

Herbs add flavour to food, and are often used in Italian cooking. Three of the most common herbs are basil, oregano and thyme. Fresh herbs often have more flavour and take less time to cook, but dried herbs can be kept for longer. Most recipes in this book use dried herbs, but suggest how to use fresh ones. A few dishes really need fresh herbs to taste their best!

Oil

Italians use olive oil, made from olives, for **frying** and for **drizzling** over pasta, salads and other dishes. You can use other kinds of oil, such as sunflower, or corn oil, but olive oil gives a more genuinely Italian flavour, so use it to make these dishes if you can.

Pasta

Pasta is made from flour, water and sometimes eggs, and is used in many Italian dishes. It comes in many different shapes, each with its own name, such as spaghetti or fusilli. Most supermarkets have a good selection of fresh and dried pasta. Dried pasta takes longer to cook, but is less expensive than fresh pasta and keeps for a long time.

Rice

Rice is the basis of a famous Italian dish called 'risotto'. Risotto is usually made with a special sort of rice called 'arborio', which gives the risotto the right creamy texture. It can be found in most supermarkets – it is often just called Italian rice or risotto rice.

Tomatoes

Tomatoes are used in many Italian dishes. In most dishes in this book, you can use either fresh or canned tomatoes.

Before you start

Kitchen rules

There are a few basic rules you
should always follow when you are cooking.

- Ask an adult if you can use the kitchen.
- Some cooking processes, especially those involving
  hot water or oil, can be dangerous. When you see
  this sign, take extra care or ask an adult to help.
- Wash your hands before you start.
- Wear an apron to protect your clothes, and tie back
  long hair.
- Be very careful when using sharp knives.
- Never leave pan handles sticking out in case you
  knock them.
- Always wear oven gloves to lift things in and out of
  the oven.
- Wash fruit and vegetables before you use them.

How long will it take?

Some of the recipes in this book are quick and easy,
and some are more difficult and take longer. The strip
across the top of the right hand page of each recipe
tells you how long it will take to cook each dish from
start to finish. It also shows how difficult each dish is
to make: every recipe is either * (easy), ** (medium) or
*** (difficult).

Quantities and measurements

You can see how many people each recipe will serve at
the top of the right hand page, too. Most of the
recipes in this book make enough to feed two people.
Where it is more sensible to make a larger amount,
though, the recipe makes enough for four.

You can multiply or divide the quantities if you want to cook for more or fewer people.

Ingredients for recipes can be measured in two different ways. Metric measurements use grams and millilitres. Imperial measurements use ounces and fluid ounces. This book uses metric measurements. If you want to convert these into imperial measurements, see the chart on page 44.

In the recipes you will see the following abbreviations:

tbsp = tablespoon   g = grams
tsp = teaspoon   ml = millilitres

Utensils

To cook the recipes in this book, you will need these utensils (as well as kitchen essentials such as spoons, plates and bowls):

- baking tray
- chopping board
- food processor
- frying pan
- grater
- ladle
- large, flat, ovenproof dish
- lemon squeezer
- measuring jug
- rolling pin
- saucepan with lid
- set of scales
- sharp knife
- sieve or colander
- whisk
- wooden cocktail sticks or skewers

(!) Whenever you use kitchen knives, be very careful.

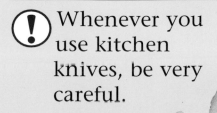

Minestrone soup

Soup is often served as a starter in Italy, although it can also be eaten as a light meal with bread. Minestrone soup is eaten all over the country, but its ingredients vary from place to place, and from season to season. In winter, more pasta is added to make a thicker, more filling soup. In summer, it might contain seasonal vegetables like asparagus and broad beans.

What you need

½ onion
1 garlic clove
1 celery stick
½ carrot
¼ cabbage
40g spaghetti
1 vegetable stock cube
1 tbsp oil
200g canned chopped tomatoes
40g canned haricot beans
1 tsp dried or a few sprigs of fresh parsley

What you do

1 **Peel** the skin from the onion and the garlic clove, and finely **chop** them.

2 Chop the celery and carrot into **slices**.

3 **Shred** the cabbage into small pieces.

4 Using your hands, break the spaghetti into small pieces, about 2cm long.

5 Put 300ml cold water into a saucepan, and bring it to the **boil**. Crumble the stock cube into the water, and stir until it **dissolves**. Put the stock to one side.

⚠ 6 Heat the oil in a saucepan over a medium heat. Add the chopped onion, garlic, celery and carrot. **Fry** for 3 minutes.

7 Add the canned tomatoes, vegetable stock, cabbage, haricot beans and parsley (if using dried parsley). Bring to the boil, then **simmer** for 10 minutes.

8 Add the broken spaghetti.

9 Cook the soup for another 8 minutes, stirring occasionally to stop it sticking to the bottom of the pan. If you are using fresh parsley, add it just before you serve the soup.

Butternut squash soup

Butternut squashes have a mild, sweet flavour. If you can't find one, use another kind of squash, such as a pumpkin. This smooth butternut squash soup is very filling.

What you need

1 butternut squash
1 onion
1 garlic clove
1 vegetable stock cube
2 tbsp oil
40g Parmesan cheese

What you do

1 Using a sharp knife, carefully cut the butternut squash in half lengthways. You only need half of the squash for this recipe.

2 Use a dessert spoon to scoop the seeds out of the squash.

3 Using the same knife, carefully **peel** off the skin, and **chop** the squash into small pieces.

4 Peel the skin from the onion and garlic clove, and finely chop them.

5 Put 500ml water into a saucepan, and bring it to the **boil**. Crumble the stock cube into the water, and stir until it **dissolves**. Put the stock to one side.

6 Heat the oil in a saucepan over a medium heat. Add the chopped onion, garlic and squash and **fry** them for 5 minutes.

7 Add the vegetable stock. Bring to the boil, then turn the heat to its lowest setting. **Simmer** the soup for 15 minutes.

8 While the soup is simmering, **grate** the Parmesan cheese.

(!) **9** Pour the soup into a food processor or blender, and **blend** until it is smooth.

10 Spoon the soup into two bowls and sprinkle grated Parmesan cheese over each.

Polenta and goats' cheese salad

Polenta is a type of flour made from ground corn. It is mixed with water, then cooked. Polenta is used in lots of dishes, especially in the north of Italy. You could serve this dish as a starter or a light meal. If you cannot find goats' cheese, you can use any type of cheese which is creamy and easy to spread.

What you need

300g 'ready to use' polenta (see page 15)
100g goats' cheese
50g mixed lettuce leaves
1 tbsp olive oil
½ tbsp balsamic vinegar or red wine vinegar

What you do

1 Cut the polenta into **slices** about ½ cm thick.

2 Put the polenta slices onto a grill pan. **Grill** them for about 7 minutes, until they start to go brown. Turn them over, and grill for another 7 minutes.

3 Take the polenta from under the grill. Spread the goats' cheese onto one side of each slice.

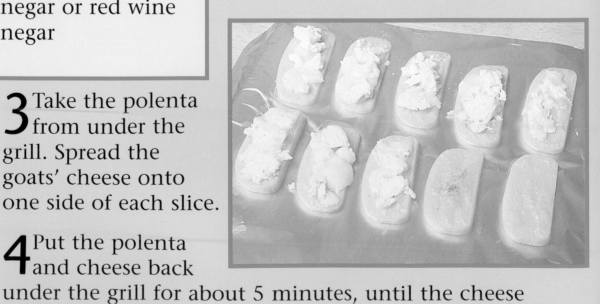

4 Put the polenta and cheese back under the grill for about 5 minutes, until the cheese starts to bubble.

5 Mix the oil and vinegar together. Put the lettuce into a bowl and add the oil and vinegar.

6 **Toss** the salad with a spoon to coat the leaves with the oil and vinegar.

7 Put the salad onto plates, and arrange the polenta slices on top.

BUYING POLENTA

You can buy polenta in two forms – as flour, or in a 'ready to use' form. Ready to use polenta is baked to form a solid cake. If you can't find this, buy polenta flour and follow the instructions on the packet to make a polenta cake to grill.

Spaghetti bolognese

In Italy, pasta dishes are often served as starters, rather than as main courses. There are over 200 different shapes of pasta. Every region has its favourite pasta, and its favourite way of serving it. Spaghetti bolognese is named after Bologna, a city in northern Italy.

What you need

1 onion
1 garlic clove
1 tbsp olive oil
75g mushrooms
250g lean minced beef
400g canned chopped
   tomatoes
½ tsp dried oregano
½ tsp dried basil
150g spaghetti

What you do

1 **Peel** the skin from the onion and the garlic clove, and finely **chop** them.

2 Cut the mushrooms into **slices**.

3 Heat the oil in a saucepan over a medium heat. Add the chopped onion and garlic, and **fry** for 5 minutes.

4 Add the minced beef, and cook for another 10 minutes, stirring occasionally, until the mince is brown.

5 Add the canned tomatoes, sliced mushrooms, oregano and basil. Stir well.

6 Reduce the heat to its lowest setting. **Cover** the pan and cook gently for 20 minutes.

7 Meanwhile, bring a saucepan of water to the **boil**. Carefully add the spaghetti and cook for about 10 minutes, until the spaghetti has just started to go soft.

(!) 8 **Drain** the spaghetti and put it into two bowls. Spoon the bolognese sauce over the spaghetti.

PASTA SHAPES

Here are some of the most common pasta shapes:

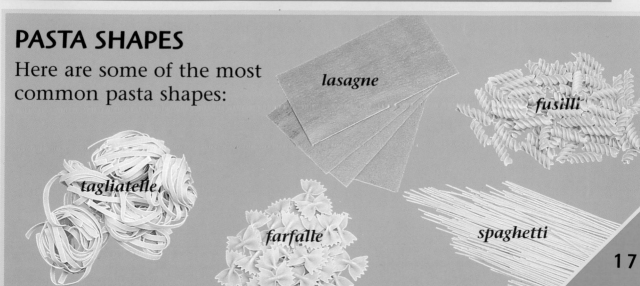

lasagne

fusilli

tagliatelle

farfalle

spaghetti

17

Pasta carbonara

Pasta carbonara was first made in Rome. It used to be seen as a poor person's meal, because in days when meat was expensive, this dish made a small amount of meat go a long way.

What you need

1 tbsp olive oil
100g smoked bacon
1 garlic clove
150g pasta shapes
   (try farfalle, penne,
   or fusilli)
4 tbsp double cream
2 egg yolks
40g Parmesan cheese

What you do

1 Using a sharp knife, cut the bacon into small pieces.

2 Peel the skin from the garlic clove, and finely **chop** it.

3 To separate the yolks from the whites, gently crack open an egg, so the shell is in two halves. Keeping the yolk in one half of the shell, let the white drip out into a bowl. Pass the yolk carefully between the two halves of the shell until all the white has dripped out. Tip the yolk into a separate bowl. Repeat this with the second egg.

4 Grate the Parmesan cheese.

5 Bring a saucepan of water to the **boil**. Add the pasta shapes, turn down the heat, and **simmer** for about 10 minutes, until the pasta has just started to go soft.

⊘ 6 While the pasta is cooking, heat the oil in a saucepan over a medium heat. Add the bacon and **fry** gently for 3 minutes.

7 Add the chopped garlic, and fry for another minute.

8 Add the cream to the egg yolks, and **beat** them with a fork. Add the cream and egg mixture to the bacon in the frying pan, and heat gently for 2 minutes, stirring all the time to make sure the egg cooks.

⊘ 9 **Drain** the pasta by emptying it into a colander or sieve. Put it into two bowls and spoon on the sauce. Sprinkle with Parmesan cheese and serve.

Lasagne

Lasagne is a pasta dish first made in northern Italy. It is **baked** in the oven. You need to make twice as much of the bolognese sauce shown on page 16, so double all the quantities shown there.

What you need

2 quantities bolognese sauce
300g lasagne pasta
30g butter or margarine
30g cornflour
600ml milk
100g Parmesan cheese

What you do

1 Follow steps 1 to 6 of the recipe on page 16, making twice the amount of bolognese sauce shown there.

2 **Grate** the Parmesan cheese.

3 **Preheat** the oven to 180°C/350°F/ gas mark 4.

4 Melt the butter or margarine in a saucepan over a low heat. Then, take the saucepan off the heat, and gradually add the cornflour, stirring all the time, to make a thick paste.

5 Keeping the pan off the heat, gradually stir the milk into the paste.

6 Put the sauce back on the heat. Stir it until it becomes thick and starts to bubble.

7 Spread one third of the bolognese sauce across the bottom of an ovenproof dish. Cover this with a layer of lasagne pasta, then spread one third of the white sauce over the pasta.

8 Repeat this process twice more, making sure the final layer of white sauce completely covers the pasta.

9 Sprinkle the grated Parmesan cheese over the top.

10 **Cover** the lasagne with foil, and bake in the oven for 20 minutes.

11 Remove the foil, and bake for another 15 minutes until the top of the lasagne is brown and bubbling.

12 Cut the lasagne into four portions, and serve.

Cheese and tomato pizza

Pizzas were first made in Naples, a city in southern Italy. This recipe tells you how to make a basic cheese and tomato pizza. You could use it as a base for adding different toppings, such as salami, ham, sliced mushrooms or sliced red peppers.

What you need

For the pizza base:
125g self-raising flour
½ tsp salt
2 tbsp olive oil
75ml warm water

For the topping:
1 onion
1 tbsp olive oil
200g canned chopped
   tomatoes
½ tsp dried oregano
½ tsp dried basil
125g mozzarella cheese

What you do

1 **Preheat** the oven to 230°C/450°F/gas mark 8.

2 Put the flour and salt in a large bowl. Add the olive oil, stirring all the time.

3 Slowly pour the warm water into the flour and oil mixture, stirring while you pour. When the water is mixed into the flour, use your hands to make the mixture into a ball.

4 Sprinkle some flour onto a chopping board. Turn the ball of pizza dough out on to the chopping board, then **knead** it until it is smooth and soft.

5 Using a rolling pin, roll out the dough into a circle about 30cm wide. Put the pizza base on to a baking tray and leave it on one side.

6 **Peel** the skin from the onion, and finely **chop** it.

(!) **7** Heat the oil in a saucepan over a medium heat. Add the onion, and **fry** for 3 minutes.

8 Add the tomatoes, oregano and basil to the saucepan. **Simmer** this tomato sauce for about 15 minutes.

9 Spoon the tomato sauce over the pizza base, spreading it out with the back of a spoon.

10 Cut the mozzarella into thin **slices** and arrange them over the top of the pizza.

11 Put the pizza into the oven, and **bake** for 10 minutes.

Potato and blue cheese calzone

Calzones are pizzas that are folded over to make half a circle. Because the filling is sealed inside the crust, they are ideal as part of a picnic. Before you start, you need to make a pizza base by following stages 2 to 5 of the pizza recipe on page 22.

What you need

1 pizza base
1 onion
200g potatoes
2 tbsp olive oil
75g blue cheese (for example Dolcelatte)
75g mozzarella cheese

What you do

1 Make a pizza base by following steps 2 to 5 of the recipe on page 22.

2 **Preheat** the oven to 230°C/450°F/gas mark 8.

3 **Peel** the skin from the onion, and finely **chop** it.

4 Peel or scrub the potatoes, and chop them into small pieces.

5 Heat the oil in a frying pan over a medium heat. Add the chopped onion and **fry** for 3 minutes.

6 Bring a pan of water to the **boil**. Add the pieces of potato and boil for about 5 minutes, until they are soft. **Drain** the water from the potatoes by emptying the pan into a colander or sieve.

7 Cut the blue cheese and mozzarella cheese into small pieces.

8 Add the cheeses and the fried onions to the potatoes, and mix together.

9 Put the pizza base onto a baking tray. Spoon the cheese and potato mixture onto half the pizza base.

10 Fold the pizza base in half so all the filling is covered. Using your fingers, press the edges of the base together to seal the filling inside.

11 Put the calzone into the oven, and **bake** for 15 minutes.

Prawn and mushroom risotto

Risotto is a traditional Italian rice dish. It is a very filling main course.

What you need

1 onion
75g mushrooms
25g Parmesan cheese
1 vegetable stock cube
1 tbsp olive oil
200g arborio rice
a few leaves fresh
    oregano or ½ tsp
    dried oregano
a few leaves fresh basil
    or ½ tsp dried basil
100g cooked prawns

What you do

1 **Peel** the skin from the onion, and finely **chop** it.

2 **Slice** the mushrooms.

3 **Grate** the Parmesan cheese.

4 Put 300ml water into a saucepan, and bring it to the **boil**. Crumble the stock cube into the water, and stir until it **dissolves**. Put the stock to one side.

(!) 5 Heat the oil in a large pan over a medium heat. Add the chopped onion, and **fry** for about 3 minutes until the onion is soft.

6 Add the rice to the pan. Cook for a further 5 minutes, stirring all the time to make sure the rice does not stick.

7 Put 3 tbsp of the vegetable stock in a ladle and add to the pan. Stir well.

8 Add the sliced mushrooms. If you are using dried herbs, add them now.

9 When the stock has been soaked up, add another 2 tbsp of stock. Keep stirring the risotto and adding more stock until the rice is soft. This should take about 20 minutes.

10 Stir in the prawns, and cook for 3 minutes.

11 Turn off the heat, then stir in the grated Parmesan cheese.

12 If you are using fresh herbs, chop the basil leaves and stir them in. Spoon the risotto onto two plates and sprinkle the oregano leaves on top.

Baked cod and potatoes

Many Italian people buy fish and seafood that is still alive from the market. This makes sure it is as fresh as possible when they start to cook it. In this dish you can use fresh or frozen fish. If you use frozen fish, make sure it is completely **thawed** before you start cooking.

What you need

200g potatoes
25g butter or
    margarine
1 tsp dried thyme
2 cod fillets
1 tbsp olive oil

What you do

1 **Preheat** the oven to 220°C/425°F/gas mark 7.

2 **Peel** or scrub the potatoes, and cut them into thin **slices**. Put them into a saucepan, and add just enough water to cover them.

(!) 3 **Boil** the potato slices in the water for 5 minutes, until they are just starting to go soft. **Drain** the water from the potatoes by emptying the pan into a colander or sieve.

4 Using your fingers, rub the butter or margarine over the bottom of an ovenproof dish.

5 Arrange the potato slices in the bottom of the dish. Sprinkle the thyme over the potatoes.

6 Put the cod fillets on top of the potatoes.

7 **Drizzle** the oil over the cod fillets.

8 Put the dish in the oven, and **bake** for 20 minutes.

ADDED OLIVES

Try adding olives to this dish, if you like them.
Put 1 tbsp of black olives (with the stones taken out)
onto the potatoes at the same time as you add the fish.

Aubergine and mozzarella towers

This **vegetarian** main course is served with 'pesto', a sauce made from fresh basil, Parmesan cheese and pine nuts. You can make your own pesto (see page 36), or buy it ready made.

What you need

1 small aubergine
1 large tomato
125g mozzarella cheese
2 tbsp pesto (see page 36)
a little olive oil

What you do

1 **Preheat** the oven to 190°C/375°F/gas mark 5.

2 Cut the aubergine into 4 **slices**. Throw the top and bottom away.

3 Put the aubergine slices onto a grill pan. **Grill** them for about 10 minutes, then turn them over and grill them on the other side for another 10 minutes.

4 Meanwhile, cut the tomato and mozzarella cheese into 4 slices.

5 Rub a small amount of oil onto a baking tray, using your fingers or a piece of kitchen roll.

6 Build the towers like this:
- Put 2 grilled aubergine slices onto the baking tray.
- Put a tomato slice on top of each aubergine slice.
- Put a mozzarella slice on top of each tomato slice.
- Add another layer of aubergine, tomato and mozzarella slices to each tower.

7 Stick a cocktail stick or a skewer through each tower to hold it together.

8 Put the towers in the oven, and **bake** for 10 minutes.

9 Take the towers out of the oven, and put them onto plates. Carefully take out the cocktail sticks or skewers.

10 Spoon the pesto over the top of the towers.

Vegetable frittata

Frittata is the Italian version of an omelette. It can be made with all sorts of vegetables. You need to use a frying pan with an ovenproof handle for this recipe, as you need to put the pan into the oven.

What you need

1 onion
1 garlic clove
1 red pepper
1 courgette
1 medium potato
3 eggs
25g Parmesan cheese
1 tbsp olive oil
1 tsp dried thyme

What you do

1 **Preheat** the oven to 200°C/400°F/gas mark 6.

2 **Peel** the skin from the onion and the garlic clove, and finely **chop** them.

3 Cut the red pepper in half. Scoop out the seeds, then chop the flesh into small pieces.

4 Cut the courgette into thin **slices**.

5 Crack the eggs into a small bowl. **Beat** them with a fork or a **whisk** until the yolk and the white are mixed.

6 **Grate** the Parmesan cheese.

7 Peel or scrub the potato. Cut it into small pieces, about 1cm across. Put the pieces of potato into a saucepan, and cover them with water.

8 **Boil** the potato pieces for 5 minutes, until they are just starting to go soft. **Drain** them by emptying the pan into a colander or sieve.

9 Heat the oil in an ovenproof frying pan over a medium heat.

⚠ **10** Add the chopped onion, garlic, red pepper, sliced courgette, cooked potato pieces and thyme to the frying pan. **Fry** for 5 minutes.

11 Pour the beaten eggs into the pan, covering all the vegetables. Cook for 3 minutes.

12 Take the pan off the heat, and sprinkle the grated Parmesan cheese over the mixture.

13 Put the pan into the oven, and cook the frittata for 15 minutes, until the egg is set and golden brown.

14 Take the pan out, run a knife around the edge and slide your frittata onto a plate. Serve it in slices.

Bruschetta

'Bruschetta' is the name for Italian garlic bread. It is made with an Italian bread called 'ciabatta', which can be found in most supermarkets. Fresh parsley tastes and looks best sprinkled on top, but if you cannot find any, use dried parsley instead. Bruschetta makes a good snack, and is also delicious served with soup.

What you need

ciabatta bread
1 garlic clove
handful of fresh parsley
   leaves
2 tbsp olive oil
salt

What you do

1 Cut the ciabatta bread into four **slices**.

2 **Peel** the skin from the garlic clove, but don't **chop** it.

3 Finely chop the fresh parsley leaves.

4 Put the slices of ciabatta on to a grill pan, and **grill** them for about 3 minutes. Turn them over, and grill for another 3 minutes on the other side. The toasted bread should be golden brown.

5 Rub the garlic clove over one side of each slice of ciabatta. The bread acts like a **grater**, so that the garlic is cut into tiny pieces and spread over the bread.

6 Sprinkle the ciabatta with the salt and chopped parsley.

7 Carefully **drizzle** the olive oil over the top. Eat your bruschetta immediately, before it goes soggy!

OTHER BREAD

If you can't find ciabatta, you could try making bruschetta with other types of crusty bread, such as slices of a long French stick, or baguette.

Pesto

'Pesto' is a sauce made from fresh basil, Parmesan cheese and pine nuts. In Italy, pesto is eaten with all sorts of dishes; it is stirred into soups, added to pasta or spooned over vegetables.

You can buy ready made pesto, but it is easy to make your own. It will keep in the fridge for up to two weeks in a clean jar with a lid.

What you need

1 garlic clove
30g fresh basil leaves
2 tbsp pine nuts
4 tbsp olive oil
30g Parmesan cheese

What you do

1 **Peel** the skin from the garlic clove.

2 Put the basil, peeled garlic clove, pine nuts and olive oil in a food processor or a blender. Make sure the lid is on properly.

3 Turn the food processor or blender up to its highest speed. **Blend** the ingredients together to make a thick, creamy sauce.

4 Pour the sauce into a bowl.

5 **Grate** the Parmesan cheese into the sauce, and stir everything together well.

PURPLE PESTO

As well as green basil, you can sometimes find basil with purple leaves. If you use purple basil to make pesto, you will have beautiful bright purple sauce to stir into pasta!

Chocolate risotto

In Italy, risotto is not always a savoury dish. Here's a recipe for a chocolate one! As with the prawn and mushroom risotto on page 26, it is best made with 'arborio' rice (often called Italian rice or risotto rice). It tastes like a delicious chocolate rice pudding.

What you need

300ml milk
15g sugar
25g butter or
   margarine
80g rice
25g sultanas
40g plain chocolate

What you do

1 **Grate** the chocolate. (This is easiest when the chocolate is very cold.)

2 Put the milk and sugar into a saucepan. Heat it over a low heat until it is hot, but not **boiling**.

3 Melt the butter or margarine in another saucepan. Add the rice, and stir well so that the rice is coated with the butter or margarine.

4 Add 2 tbsp of the hot milk to the rice, and stir it in.

5 When the milk has been soaked up, add a further 2 tbsp milk. Keep stirring the risotto and adding more milk until the rice is soft. This should take about 20 minutes.

6 Stir all the sultanas and almost all the grated chocolate into the risotto.

7 Divide the risotto into two bowls, and sprinkle them with the chocolate you have left.

SWEET RISOTTOS

Why not try experimenting with other sweet risottos? Instead of the grated chocolate, you could try adding honey, jam or chopped dried apricots.

Vanilla ice cream

Italy is famous for its ice cream. It is easy to make your own, but you need to stir it regularly while it freezes, to stop lumps of ice forming.

What you need

300ml milk
1 tsp vanilla essence
4 egg yolks
100g caster sugar
300ml double cream

What you do

1 Put the milk and vanilla essence into a saucepan. Heat over a low heat until it is hot, but not **boiling**.

2 To separate the egg yolks from the whites, carefully crack open an egg. Keep the yolk in one half of the shell, let the white drip out into a bowl. Pass the yolk between the two halves of the shell until all the white has dripped out. Tip the yolk into a separate bowl. Repeat this with the other three eggs.

3 Add the sugar to the bowl of egg yolks. **Beat** the egg yolks and sugar together until they are well mixed.

(!) 4 Gradually add the hot milk into the egg and sugar mixture, stirring all the time.

5 Carefully pour the mixture back into the saucepan. Cook it over a low heat until it thickens, stirring all the time.

6 Pour the mixture into a bowl, then stir in the cream.

7 Put the mixture into the freezer. After an hour, take the bowl out and **mash** the mixture with a fork to break up any lumps.

8 Mash the ice cream every hour until it is set. This should take about 4 to 5 hours, depending on how cold your freezer is.

OTHER FLAVOURS

In Italy, there are countless flavours of ice cream.
Why not try making up your own flavours by adding extra ingredients such as chocolate chips or mashed strawberries to the mixture at the same time as the cream?

Lemon granita

'Granita' is a frozen fruit pudding. It has tiny granules of ice in it, which is how it got its name. In Italy it is often served topped with whipped cream and accompanied by a sweet pastry. Granita is easy to make, and very refreshing.

What you need

2 lemons
50g sugar

What you do

1 Put the sugar into a saucepan with 300ml water. Bring the mixture to the **boil**, stirring until all the sugar **dissolves**. Boil for 5 minutes.

2 Leave the sugar and water mixture to **cool**.

3 Using a lemon squeezer, squeeze the juice out of the lemons into a bowl.

4 Add the cooled sugar and water mixture to the lemon juice. Stir well.

5 Put the bowl into the freezer. After an hour, take the bowl out of the freezer, and **mash** the mixture with a fork to break up any big lumps.

6 Put the bowl back into the freezer. After another hour, take it out of the freezer, and mash it again with a fork before you serve it.

VARIATIONS

You can make granita with other types of fruit. Try replacing the lemon juice with the juice from oranges or grapefruits, or with mashed strawberries.

Further information

Here are some places to find out more about Italy and Italian cooking.

Books

Cooking the Italian Way
Alphonse Bisignano, Lerner Publications, 1982
Food in Italy
Claudia Gaspari, The Rourke Book Company, 1989
A Taste of Italy
Jenny Ridgewell, Thomson Learning, 1993
Next Stop: Italy
Fred Martin, Heinemann Library, 1998

Websites

www.italy1.com/cuisine/english
soar.berkeley.edu/recipes/ethnic/italian
www.astray.com/recipes/?search=italian
www.thevision.net/DMS/galley.htm#italian
www.yumyum.com/recipes/htm

Conversion chart

Ingredients for recipes can be measured in two different ways. Metric measurements use grams and millilitres. Imperial measurements use ounces and fluid ounces. This book uses metric measurements. The chart here shows you how to convert measurements from metric to imperial.

SOLIDS		LIQUIDS	
METRIC	IMPERIAL	METRIC	IMPERIAL
10g	¼ oz	30ml	1 fl oz
15g	½ oz	50ml	2 fl oz
25g	1 oz	75ml	2½ fl oz
50g	1¾ oz	100ml	3½ fl oz
75g	2¾ oz	125ml	4 fl oz
100g	3½ oz	150ml	5 fl oz
150g	5 oz	300ml	10 fl oz
250g	9 oz	600ml	20 fl oz

Healthy eating

This diagram shows which foods you should eat to stay healthy. Most of your food should come from the bottom of the pyramid. Eat some of the foods from the middle every day. Only eat a little of the foods from the top.

Healthy eating Italian Style

Italian food includes lots of pasta and some rice, which belong to the bottom layer, along with bread and pizza dough. Italian people also eat lots of fresh vegetables, as well as some meat and fish. Many of their desserts are made with fruit so you can see how healthy Italian cooking is!

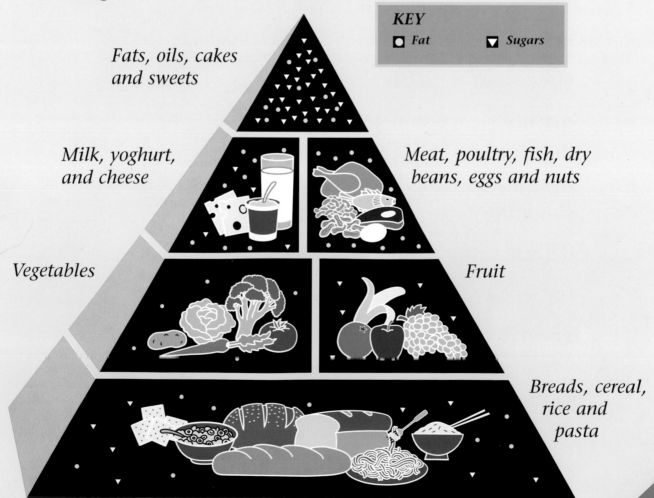

Fats, oils, cakes and sweets

KEY
☐ *Fat*   ▽ *Sugars*

Milk, yoghurt, and cheese

Meat, poultry, fish, dry beans, eggs and nuts

Vegetables

Fruit

Breads, cereal, rice and pasta

Glossary

bake cook something in the oven

beat mix something together strongly, for example egg yolks and whites

blend mix ingredients together in a blender or food processor

boil cook a liquid on the hob. Boiling liquid bubbles and steams strongly.

chop cut something into pieces using a knife

cool allow hot food to become cold. You should always allow food to cool before putting it in the fridge.

cover put a lid on a pan, or foil over a dish

dissolve mix something, for example sugar, until it disappears into a liquid

drain remove liquid, usually by pouring something into a colander or sieve

drizzle pour something very slowly and evenly

fry cook something in oil in a pan

grains foods like wheat, maize and rice. They are the seeds of cereal plants.

grate break something, for example cheese, into small pieces using a grater

grill cook something under the grill

knead mix ingredients into a smooth dough, for example for bread. You use your hand to push the dough away from you.

mash crush something, for example potatoes, until it is soft and pulpy

peel remove the skin of a fruit or vegetable

preheat turn on the oven in advance, so that it is hot when you are ready to use it

Roman Empire period in history from around 100 BC–400 AD. The Romans conquered much of Europe, and parts of Asia and north Africa.

shred cut or tear something, for example a lettuce, into small pieces

simmer cook a liquid on the hob. Simmering liquid bubbles and steams gently.

slice cut something into thin, flat pieces

thaw defrost something which has been frozen

toss mix ingredients, for example in a salad quite roughly

vegetarian food that does not contain meat, or fish. People who don't eat meat or fish are called vegetarians.

whisk mix ingredients using a whisk

Index